A LITTLE
HISTORY
OF GOLF

KIM LENAGHAN   Illustrated by HELEN AVERLEY

CHRONICLE BOOKS
SAN FRANCISCO

First published in 1996 by
Appletree Press
19-21 Alfred Street
Belfast BT2 8DL

Text and illustrations © Appletree Press, 1996

Printed in the U.A.E.

First published in the United States in 1996 by
Chronicle Books, 275 Fifth Street, San Francisco,
California, 94103.

ISBN 0-8118-1266-9

9 8 7 6 5 4 3 2 1

Contents

Definition of Golf

"To hit a very small ball into an even smaller hole, with weapons singularly ill designed for the purpose".

Winston Churchill

Jeu de mail

The Origins of Golf

❦

The game of golf, or something like it, has been played for centuries, but its actual origins are somewhat shrouded in mystery. While Scotland is generally accepted as being the cradle of golf, a number of other European stick-and-ball games would lay claim to being its illustrious forbearer.

The word golf probably derives from the German *kolb* meaning club, but some historians suggest that the sport actually dates back as far as Ancient Rome. **Paganica,** a game played in the halcyon days of the Roman Empire, employed a bent stick and a leather ball stuffed with feathers. In the first century B.C., the Romans began their invasion of Europe, bringing their popular pastime of paganica with them. The game became very popular, particularly in regions that eventually formed the countries Holland, Belgium, and France, where it formed the basis for many other games now considered to be the possible originators of golf.

Certainly a game quite similar to golf was played in Holland.

Called **kolf** or **kolven,** the game probably bears less similarity to golf than the name itself. Though sometimes played outside on ice, **kolven** was essentially an indoor game played on a smooth wooden floor in a rectangular area 60 x 25 feet (18 x 7.5m), with a post about 5 inches (12cm) in diameter placed about 8-10 feet (25 x 3m) from each end wall. Using clubs with straight shafts about 4 feet (1.25m) long, the players attempted to knock a leather ball the size of a cricket ball from one end of the court to the other, hit the posts, and bring it to rest as close to the wall as possible in the fewest number of strokes. In the case of a tie in the number of shots, the winner was the one whose ball was closest to the wall. Ultimately, this game was more akin to billiards and croquet than golf. Based more on skill than power, kolven is perhaps a more likely antecedent for hockey or ice hockey.

Another game that owes something to paganica was the French **jeu de mail**. Using a *mail*, a kind of wooden mallet, the players struck wooden balls over a designated course about one-half mile long to a fixed spot or landmark. They counted the number of strokes taken to reach the target, and the winner was whoever took the least strokes to complete the course. Another similarity to golf was that each player could hit only their own ball.

In Belgium, a later version of jeu de mail was the Flemish game of **chole**, which dates to the mid-fourteenth century. This was played cross-country between predetermined starting

Kolven

and finishing points, with the object to reach the end of the course in a specified number of strokes. The implements for the game were clubs with long wooden handles and large iron heads which were used to strike an egg-shaped ball made from beechwood or leather.

One team would try to make the target within the declared number of shots, while their opponents tried to prevent them. First, the offensive side would play three strokes to move the ball toward the finish, then a member of the defensive team was allowed to hit the ball as far back as possible or into any awkward obstacle that would impede the progress of their rivals. This backward stroke was called a *decholade*. The game continued, three stokes forward and one stroke back, to its conclusion.

Pell mell was another game, similar in concept to jeu de mail, that was introduced to England and Scotland from France in the sixteenth century. Mary, Queen of Scots, is recorded as having played pell mell, and, later on, Charles I was a devotee. The English translation is "pall mall." This was the name given to the original course laid out in London. The area still bears the name, though now it is a busy thoroughfare.

An earlier game played in England, during the reign of Edward III, was **cambuca.** Using a curved club, a player struck a ball made from feathers towards a pin in the ground in an action a little like hockey. The game was so popular that it was actually banned from feast day activities in 1363, to encourage the able-bodied men of the population to practice their archery.

In England's Gloucester Cathedral a stained-glass window, dating back to the 1300s, features scenes from the Battle of Crécy in France. One image depicts a figure swinging a curved club. This is most often referred to as "the golfer," but the game being played was more likely to be cambuca.

But what of the Scots? It has been suggested that the game of kolf was introduced to Scotland from Holland through trading links between the two countries that had been in existence since medieval times. This theory is supported by the fact that until well into the nineteenth century golf in Scotland was confined to the east coast. If the game had originated in that country, it would have enjoyed a larger geographic spread. Also, the earliest documented reference to golf in Holland dates from

1360, but in Scotland there is no mention until 1457. Given this evidence it would seem that the Dutch introduced the game of kolf to the Scots after all.

However, this theory overlooks one key aspect of golf. There is no record in any of the documentation on these supposed golfing forbearers of that most basic element in golf: the use of a hole in the ground. While all these early stick-and-ball games have similarities to golf, all the targets used were

above the ground. It was in Scotland that the hole made its first appearance in the game, surely proving that Scotland is indeed the home of golf.

St Andrews

The Scottish Influence

❦

There is no doubt that even if they did not invent golf the Scots were the true pioneers of the game. The Old Course at St. Andrews lays claim to being the birthplace of the game and is undoubtedly the oldest links in the world in continuous use as a golf course, though there is an argument that it was in fact predated by Leith.

Wherever it was first played, golf was a significant Scottish pastime from the beginning of the fourteenth century, though the earliest recorded evidence of its popularity in Scotland dates back to 1457. In that year King James II banned the playing of "golfe and fut ball" by a Scottish Act of Parliament because he feared it was interfering with the practice of archery, the bow being the main weapon of warfare at the time.

However, the king's warnings fell on deaf ears, and the Scots played on. So, after James IV acceded to the throne, a stiffer law was passed in 1491. This new law set a hefty fine and prison for anyone caught playing the game, an unpopular move not just with the masses but also with the nobility who were known to be devotees of the sport. Perhaps it was they who led the king to have something of a change of heart, because ultimately he became a fan of the sport he had tried to ban.

After James' conversion, the Scottish royals openly did an about face, and in the mid-sixteenth century golf became the object of royal patronage. James V was a fan of the game, passing on his love of the sport to his ill-fated daughter, Mary, Queen of Scots. She learned to play at an early age and continued her hobby even while being educated in France. Apparently while there she christened the students who carried her clubs "cadets." Given the French pronunciation of the word (cad-day), popular belief would have it that this is how the modern term "caddie" developed.

History tells us that Mary was a dedicated golfer who played at every opportunity. In 1567 she fell foul of the church for playing a round of golf just a few days after the murder of her husband Lord Darnley! It was also during Queen Mary's reign that St. Andrews first came into existence; the citizens of the town were granted the right to use the links for golf by a charter in 1522.

Some years after her execution, Mary's son, James VI, ascended to the throne of England and Scotland. He shared the golfing passion of his ancestors and is credited with introducing the game to England. A seven-hole course was laid out on the sandy ground of Blackheath Common in 1608.

Such royal patronage was to continue through the centuries, but golf proved less popular with the Scottish church. It seems that in some cases parishioners could face punishments, including excommunication, for indulging in their favorite pastime. Despite all this, the popularity of the game increased and spread: by the seventeenth century the game was being played throughout the land.

By the middle of the eighteenth century it became apparent that there was a need for standarization, and clubs and societies devoted exclusively to golf were developed along with a universal set of rules.

The earliest recorded club was the Gentlemen Golfers of Leith (later to become the Honourable Company of Edinburgh Golfers). Founded in 1744, this small group of enthusiasts

Scottish coastal course

played on the five holes of the Leith links until the 1820s when the company disbanded. It was re-formed in 1836 and moved to Musselburgh where it stayed until 1891. The club then moved to Muirfield where it constructed the great championship links, which is still the home of the club.

Most important, the Honourable Company laid down the game's original set of thirteen rules, the Articles and Laws in Playing at Golf. These were devised by the club's first captain, Duncan Forbes, and his fellow members to allow a structure for competitions.

On May 14, 1754 twenty-two gentlemen formed the Society of St. Andrews Golfers. Then in 1834, William IV conferred upon it the title of "Royal and Ancient" and became its patron. As the century wore on, St. Andrews became the accepted home of golf, as it still is today. The Royal and Ancient was highly influential in the development of the game, decreeing that a 4½ inch (11.25cm) diameter for the hole was mandatory and stipulating that eighteen holes should constitute a match. In 1897 the Royal and Ancient was requested to update the code of play developed in Leith. It compiled the definitive set of rules recognizable to today's golfer.

Other notable clubs coming into existence at this time included Musselburgh, the Edinburgh Burgess Golfing Society, the Bruntsfield Links Golf Club, and the Glasgow Club. But the majority of the famous clubs were inaugurated in the nineteenth century, particularly in that century's last three decades.

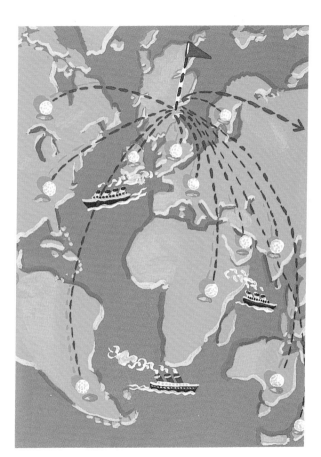

Golf Worldwide

❦

The first expansion for golf was from Scotland into the rest of Britain. In 1864 there were around thirty golf clubs in Scotland and only three in England, but by the turn of the century this situation was completely reversed. Of the 2,000 plus British clubs in existence, the majority were south of the border.

Of course, they did not all have their own courses, and in most cases one course was shared by several clubs. Naturally, Scottish professionals were imported south of the border to lay out courses and teach golf at the new clubs.

Just as the Scots brought golf to the rest of Britain, so too did they introduce the game further afield. Wherever pioneering expatriate Scots settled, they took their game with them. Among those overseas countries where they made their new home, none embraced the game of golf with quite the same enthusiasm as the United States.

The Scottish regiments who fought during the American

War of Independence, which began in 1775, played golf in their free time. But it was a century later before it really took hold under the guiding hand of John Reid, the man credited as being "the father of American golf."

John Reid and Robert Lockhart had left their homes in Dunfermline in Fife and settled on the east coast of the United States. Reid lived in Yonkers and managed an iron works, while Lockhart was a New York linen merchant who often had occasion to go back to Scotland on business trips. On one such trip, in 1887, he visited Old Tom Morris' shop at St. Andrews and ordered six clubs and two dozen gutta percha balls on behalf of his friend John Reid.

When the clubs arrived, Reid got together a group of five friends—Harry Holbrook, Alexander P.W. Kinnan, Kingham H. Putman, Henry O. Tallmadge, and John B. Upham—and took them to a cow pasture near his Yonkers home. There they laid out three short holes and built America's first-ever golf course.

Reid and his friends were hooked, ordering more equipment from Scotland and searching out a new and better location. They eventually found a thirty-acre site at North Broadway and Shonnard Place, where they laid out a rough course of six holes with greens about 12 feet (3.5m) in diameter. They played at every opportunity, particularly on Sundays, which led to their being sharply criticized by local clergy for desecrating the Sabbath, but just as their forbearers in seventeenth century Scotland had, they ignored the warnings and

John Reid

played on. On November 14, 1888, Reid gave a dinner party
for his golfing partners. During the course of the evening, they
formed the St. Andrews Club of Yonkers. Reid became president of the new club, Upham secretary/treasurer, and Robert
Lockhart, who had brought those first clubs from Scotland, was
elected as a member.

In the spring of 1892 the club moved one-half mile up the
road to a thirty-four acre apple orchard. They laid out a new
six-hole course measuring 300 feet (92m) in length. A large
tree beside the home green became an unofficial club house. As
a result the Yonkers golfers became known as the "Apple Tree
Gang."

While the members of the "Apple Tree Gang" undoubtedly

laid the foundations for golfing in America, the game captured the public imagination, and it wasn't long before they were joined by other clubs. In Middlesborough, Kentucky, a group of Englishmen constructed a nine-hole course and formed the Middlesboro Club in 1889. By 1894 there were several courses of six- and nine-holes. The floodgates were open, and

by the turn of the century there were more than 1,000 golf clubs in the United States.

The first eighteen-hole course was laid out in Chicago by Charles Blair MacDonald. He had become a devotee of the game while studying at St. Andrews University in Scotland. On his return to the USA he persuaded his friends to build a nine-hole course in suburban Belmont in 1892, adding a further nine holes a year later. Seeing the merits of a longer course, the club then moved to a new eighteen-hole layout in a beautiful 200-acre setting in Wheaton, twenty-five miles from Chicago, a site that was to become one of America's great courses.

MacDonald was a purist when it came to the rules of the game, and was instrumental in laying down the laws of U.S. golf. He was also a superb golfer and in 1895 became the first official U.S. amateur champion.

Elsewhere on the American continent, Canada had also been influenced by those wandering, golfing Scots. The first club there was founded at Montreal in 1873, quite some time before John Reid's exploits. The Royal Quebec Club was formed in 1875 and competed in the country's first inter-club match against the Royal Montreal at Cove Fields in 1876. However, the spread of golf in Canada was slower than its neighbor, perhaps due to the smaller population and colder climate, though it has become a popular sport today.

Golf spread throughout the rest of the world with the nineteenth century expansion of the British Empire. The Royal Calcutta Club in India is one of the oldest clubs in existence, founded in 1829 by Scottish golfing enthusiasts involved in trade with India. By the end of the century there were many other clubs across Asia. In 1892, the Royal Calcutta Club inaugurated the Amateur Championship of the Far East.

The sport continued to grow, and by the end of the Second World War, golf was universally acknowledged as the world's most popular sport.

The Necessary Equipment

❦

Of all the equipment necessary for playing golf, the ball has had the single greatest effect on the direction of the game, from club design to financial accessibility. The earliest balls were made from wood, generally beech, but by the sixteenth century these had been replaced by the **feathery**. Despite being expensive to buy, easily damaged, and difficult to make, these balls remained popular until the middle of the nineteenth century. They were handmade from leather and stuffed with boiled feathers. Even the most experienced ballmaker could only produce four a day. This added greatly to the price, with balls costing more than a week's wages for many enthusiastic golfers. Among the best renowned of the early makers of featheries were the Gourlay family of Leith and Musselburgh and Allan Robertson of St. Andrews.

Apart from the obvious drawback of cost, there were other problems with the feathery: it was impossible to get a perfectly round ball, and the balls were soon knocked out of shape by wooden clubs or split in wet weather. Despite this, the balls were used exclusively until 1848 and the arrival of gutta percha.

Gutta percha was a black, rubber-like substance obtained by tapping certain tropical trees in India and Asia. It was found to be soft and pliable when boiled in water and was easily pressed into the shape of a ball. It also kept its shape and hardened when cool. If broken it could be remolded on heating. The **guttie** was the ideal candidate to replace the feathery: it was considerably cheaper, longer lasting, and could be made more quickly and in much larger quantities.

The balls could also be more easily standardized. Makers stamped the weight (about one-third ounce) along with their name on each ball. The best known balls of the time carried

the brands of Old Tom Morris, Robert Forgan, and the Auchterlonies. Gutties were also the first balls to feature the distinctive striations, later developed as dimples on the modern golf ball. The guttie was king of balls until the turn of the century when, like the feathery, it fell victim to progress and was made obsolete by Haskell's revolutionary rubber ball.

Coburn Haskell was a wealthy American amateur golfer who was certain that a livelier ball than the guttie could be produced. In collaboration with Bertram G. Work of the Goodrich Rubber Company of Akron, Ohio he developed a ball made from winding rubber thread under tension around a solid rubber core. The new rubber balls were placed on the market in 1899, but they were not an immediate hit. While they travelled farther off the tee, they were hard to control on the greens, earning them the nickname of "bounding billies."

However, the creation of an automatic winding machine coupled with the use of a pattern of bramble markings improved the flight of the balls. The final seal of approval came in 1901, when Walter J. Travis won the U.S. Amateur Championship using a Haskell. All doubts about the new ball's liveliness on the greens were sensationally silenced, and it went into mass production.

We know more about aerodynamics today than our ancestors did a century ago. As a result the surface patterns of the 1900s have been replaced by the distinctive dimples that accentuate the effects of lift and minimize the amount of drag on the ball. Modern technology has also made balls consistently cheaper and of a uniform size. In 1921 the United States Golf Association and the Royal and Ancient agreed that all balls should be 1.62 inches (4cm) in diameter. A decade later the

United States Golf Association increased the size to 1.68 inches (4.2cm). Finally, in 1987, this measurement was also accepted by the Royal and Ancient and the American size is now the standard.

The quest for the perfect golf ball may have taken centuries, but the development of the perfect club is as old as the game itself. The earliest golf clubs, dating back to the fifteenth century, were fairly rudimentary, just a solid wooden shaft, a weighted head, and a padded handle bound with animal hide. It was not until the beginning of the eighteenth century that metal-headed clubs made an appearance.

The long-nosed, long-shafted playclub dominated golf in the eighteenth and nineteenth centuries. By the mid-1800s clubs could be divided into four categories: drivers, spoons, irons, and putters. There were two sorts of drivers–the **playclub driver**, which had a flat face, no loft, and was designed to hit a ball off a tee, and the **grassed driver**, slightly lofted to lift the ball from a hazard or downhill lie. There were four types of spoons–long, middle, short, and baffing. The **baffy**, as it was known, was short and stiff with a laid-back face and was used for pitching to the green. The wooden **niblick** was short, well lofted, and made with a small head so that it could cut through heavy grass. Wooden putters were used for centuries and were ideal on rougher greens. As the playing surfaces improved, the smoother, iron blade became the popular choice.

The early irons were very heavy, rather fearsome looking,

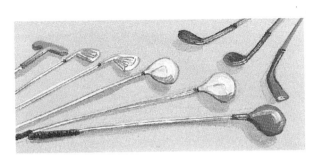

and ideal for the big hitters. They were hand forged with a sock
et into which the finely tapered shaft was fitted and driven into
the club head to give a tight fit. Initially irons were not widely
used because of the delicate nature of the feather balls, but by
the mid-nineteenth century with the advent of the gutta percha
and rubber balls they came into their own.

The heads of the wooden clubs were made mostly from
fruitwoods: hornbeam, thornwood, beech, and persimmon, a
wood imported from North America. The shafts were joined to
the underside of the neck of the clubhead by a simple splice and
held tightly using a tarred twine binding. These shafts, made
from ash, hazel, and hickory, were slender and finely tapered to
ensure the "spring" was in the right position. The grips were
made of stuff strips covered with leather and nailed to the shaft.

The arrival of the guttie had a marked effect on clubs which
became shorter, broader, and deeper with new clubs like the

bulger being developed. This was a driver with a distinctive convex face designed to minimize a sliced or hooked stroke. Another new club was the **brassie**, which took its name from its brass sole and was designed to play off hard surfaces. Iron clubs also increased in popularity, primarily because they were cheaper to manufacture and, as has already been mentioned, could not harm the new style balls.

By the turn of the century a set of irons, each with a different degree of loft, comprised the driving cleek; iron cleek; lofter; mashie; sand iron; niblick; and putting cleek. Clubs with aluminium heads made their first appearance during this period, first as putters and then as a full range of clubs.

The most significant advance in the early part of the twentieth century was the introduction of the steel shaft. The first seamless, steel shafts were produced in Britain in 1912. During the next two decades steel also became widely used in the

United States. Nevertheless, it was only in 1929 that the Royal and Ancient legalized the use of steel shafts, and only then because the Prince of Wales, later the abdicating Edward VIII, played with a set of steel shafted clubs at St. Andrews. It seemed the club had little choice but to accede to the wishes of their future king.

Mass-produced clubs followed and with them came matched sets with numbered rather than named clubs. Soon there were clubs for every possible situation, and some golfers were carrying huge numbers of clubs on each round. To combat this and force the golfer to rely once more on skill and not just clubs, the United States Golfing Association imposed a fourteen club limit in 1938, and the Royal and Ancient took similar action a year later.

Recently, most manufacturers have geared production toward game improvement with inventions like peripherally-weighted irons and customized clubs that are now widely available. Steel is still the main constituent in making shafts for irons, but carbon fibre or graphite is becoming a more popular choice because of its light weight and high strength. It is also increasingly being used for clubheads.

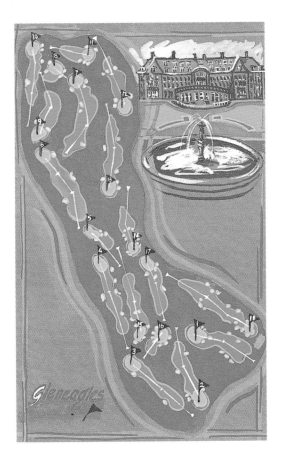

Gleneagles course

On Course

❧

T he greatest course architect of all time is nature. Its glorious early links, cut in great swathes of coast and dunes, are among its finest achievements, particularly at the birthplace of golf on the east coast of Scotland. But nature couldn't keep pace with the passion for golf, and some human intervention was required.

Early courses were laid out within one day. These were very simply designed with the links land transformed into a golf course by cutting holes, marking greens with colored stakes, and excavating bunkers in accordance with the natural terrain.

Until golf course architecture became a profession at the end of the nineteenth century, these courses were not always satisfactory. Dr. Alister Mackenzie, the great golf architect who collaborated in the creation of Augusta National in the United States, suggested in 1920: "I believe the real reason St. Andrews Old Course is infinitely superior to anything else is owing to the fact that it was constructed when no one knew anything about the subject at all, and since then it has been considered too sacred to be touched."

The desire to appear natural was as important one hundred years ago as it is now. Indeed, it was originally believed that only naturally well-endowed links courses were truly suitable for the playing of golf. That was before the efforts of the last century's army of talented architects, led by Old Tom Morris. He was one of the greatest golf professionals of his day, and the courses he laid out are legendary. His approach was simple, though he used a great deal of imagination trying to avoid the standard nine holes out and nine holes back. This is particularly notable in the courses he designed at Muirfield in Scotland and Royal County Down in Northern Ireland.

That was all very well with such fine raw material, but many of the early parkland courses were appalling. Arch critic Alister Mackenzie again did a great job of summing up their faults: "Golf, on a good links is, in all probability, the best game in the world, but on the late-Victorian type of inland course, where there is a complete lack of variety, flat fairways, flat unguarded greens, long grass, necessitating frequent searching for lost balls, and mathematically placed hazards consisting of the cop or pimple variety, it not only offends all the finest instincts of the artist and sportsman, but it is the most boring game in existence."

But all this changed with the realization that the best turf for golf courses was the least suitable for farming. The sandy sub-

soil of the heathlands to the south and west of London was the perfect foundation for a golf course. It highlighted the way forward for the development of inland sites. This was proven by pioneering golf professional Willie Park, Junior, son of the first Open champion and twice a winner himself, who laid out the first course at Sunningdale in the 1890s. His lead was followed by other golf professionals like Harry Colt, who laid out the New Course at Sunningdale, and five times Open winner, James Braid, who designed the courses at Gleneagles.

Across the Atlantic, in 1902, Charles Blair MacDonald, architect of the Chicago golf-course, began researching British golf courses. The studies assisted him greatly in designing the renowned National Golf Course. His example inspired other architects like George Crump, A.W. Tillinghast, and Hugh Wilson to create the courses at Pine Valley, Baltusrol,

Jack Nicklaus

and Merion. Donald Ross, a Scot, designed some legendary courses in the United States, among them Pinehurst Number 2. Fellow Scot Alister Mackenzie partnered with Bobby Jones in creating Augusta National. The strategic approach used for these courses revolutionized course design in the United States.

Following his somewhat controversial adaptation of the Oakland Hills course in Michigan for the 1951 U.S. Open, Robert Trent Jones became the leading golf course architect in the United States. During the 1960s and 1970s his trademark lakes amid massive bunkers were stamped on courses across the country.

In the late 1960s, Pete Dye teamed up with professional golfer Jack Nicklaus to develop the Harbour Town Golf Links in South Carolina. The two have gone on to become the best course designers in the late twentieth century. As in the early days, golf professionals are once again dominating the field of golf course design. Arnold Palmer, Seve Ballesteros, Bernhard Langer, and Tony Jacklin, to name only a few, are putting their mark and their name on courses around the globe. And there is a steady demand for more of the same.

Letting in the Ladies

❧

Until recently, women's golf has not attracted the same interest as men's, particularly on the professional circuit, although women have been playing the game for just as long.

We know that Mary, Queen of Scots and many of her female nobility were ardent golfers, but from the sixteenth century on there seems to be only scant reference to women's role in the game. Perhaps as the game developed and became more strenuous it may not have seemed quite "ladylike" enough. Add to this some of the ridiculous and restrictive fashions worn by women in the last three centuries and the playing of most active sports, not just golf, must have been virtually impossible. To cap it all, along came the golf club which, until relatively recently, was generally an all-male preserve with women strictly forbidden.

Despite all this, a few well-heeled ladies did take up the sport in the nineteenth century, but in a rather limited way.

Glenna Collet

It was considered somewhat indelicate to raise a club above shoulder height, not that their full skirts and corsets would have allowed that in any case, and balls were merely struck along the ground, not unlike croquet.

Things were changing though and women began to form their own clubs and develop a more suitable attire. In 1893 the Ladies Golf Union was formed in Britain and blossomed under the direction of its secretary Issette Pearson, a keen golfer and runner-up to Lady Margaret Scott in the first British Ladies' Amateur Championship held that same year.

Times were changing on the other side of the Atlantic too, where members of New York's Shinnecock Hills Club were persuaded by their wives to build them their own nine-hole course. By 1894 a group of female golfers had founded their own club and created a seven-hole course in Morristown, New Jersey.

The first big name in women's golf in Britain was Cecil (short for Cecilia) Leitch. When she was just seventeen she reached the semi-finals of the 1908 British Ladies' Amateur and went on to dominate the ladies' game, winning twelve titles in Britain, Canada, and France. Her trademark swing – forceful and flat – was in direct contrast to that of Joyce Wethered (Lady Heathcoat-Amory) who was noted for her elegant, stylish swing, admired by male as well as female golfers. Wethered's record in competitive golf was outstanding: she scooped five consecutive English Ladies' Championships from 1920 to 1924. She retired in 1925 but made a comeback four years later to win the British Ladies' title for a fourth time, beating U.S. Ladies' Champion Glenna Collet.

Just as Wethered dominated the game in Britain, so Collet did in the United States where she won the Women's Amateur Championship six times, a record for USGA competitions. Between 1928 and 1931, Collett won no less than nineteen consecutive matches – a feat which is as yet unbeaten.

International golf for women began in 1905 when a team from America came to play in the British Ladies' Amateur. The first international women's trophy was the Curtis Cup. The trophy was donated by Harriot and Margaret Curtis, two sisters who had played in the original international event in 1905.

America won the first Curtis Cup match in 1932 and dominated the event in subsequent years with a few notable British exceptions including a dramatic win at Prairie Dunes in 1986 that ended a run of thirteen successive American victories.

Women's golf remained largely amateur until 1949 when the Ladies' Professional Golf Association was created in the United States by Patty Berg and Babe Zaharias, two of the major players of the period.

Patty Berg was an enormously talented player whose career records successes in all the major events of the day. She was also a superb ambassador for the women's games as her bubbly personality and good looks drew attention to the sport. It therefore was only right that it should be Berg who became the first president of the USLPGA.

Babe Zaharias, the other founder member of the LPGA, was an equally remarkable golfer. She took up the sport in 1934 at the age of eighteen and immediately impressed fans of the game with her natural prowess.

An all-round athlete, Zaharias also won three Olympic gold medals in 1932, in the javelin, 80 meter hurdles and the high jump. She was also a professional baseball and basketball player. Between 1946 and 1947, Babe won seventeen competitions including the British Ladies' Amateur, making her the first American to win the title.

Berg and Zaharias led the way and were followed by such outstanding players as Mickey Wright in the 1950s Kathy

Patty Berg and Babe Zaharias

Whitworth, and Nancy Lopez, who in the 1970s, became the first woman golfing superstar.

Lopez has had an amazing career to date. Her achievements include winning the New Mexico Amateur in 1969 at the age of twelve. In 1975 she was runner-up in the U.S. Women's Open. Renowned for her unusual swing, which has variously been described as "loopy," "shut," and "faulty," Lopez went from strength to strength, winning seventeen of her first fifty tournaments on the professional circuit. In only five years she collected over $1 million in prize money and by 1989 this figure had risen to over $3 million.

No doubt the increase in the size of the purse for the women's tournaments was largely because golf had become big business, with extensive television coverage and major sponsorship deals.

The Americans dominated their home circuit for many years with most of the major trophies going to local players. One notable exception being Catherine Lacoste of France who, in 1967 at the age of twenty-two, became the youngest ever winner of the U.S. Women's Open. However, the European players did begin to catch up. A Tour of Britain and Europe has subsequently been established. One of the leading lights is British player Laura Davies who became the first Briton to win the U.S. Women's Open in 1987.

Davies is a wonderful example of a natural player. She has never had a formal lesson but has managed nevertheless to dominate the women's game in recent years. Her obvious strength lies in the power she is able to apply to her swing, often hitting the ball further than her male counterparts. Though she believes her greatest gift is the accuracy of her short game. In 1988 she won events on five separate tours—three in Europe, two in the United States and one each in Thailand, Japan, and Australia. Her influence on her teammates in the Solheim Cup – a tournament equivalent to the Ryder that has been in operation since 1990 – is considerable as her American opponents recognize her to be a formidable adversary.

Women's golf is flourishing, and the future of the game, for both amateur and professional players, looks very promising.

Laura Davies winning 1987 US Open

The Professionals

❦

Professional golfers are among the best known and most popular sporting heroes of the twentieth century, but it wasn't always so. Until about a hundred years ago, golf was very much an amateur sport, and the professionals involved in it were there to make clubs and balls, give lessons to the club members, and even carry their bags!

In the 1890s three legendary British golfers ushered in the new era of the professional golfer and played competitive golf internationally to earn a living. Harry Vardon, James Braid, and J.H. Taylor dominated the game for two decades and became known as the "Great Triumvirate."

Harry Vardon was the leading member of that outstanding trio. He is credited with inventing the "Vardon grip" – the style of grip still used by today's professionals – which involves overlapping the index finger of the left hand with the little finger of the right. It is actually more likely that Vardon merely popularized the grip, as it was used by several players of the period.

Vardon's swing, however, was quite unique. He played with his left arm bent slightly when common practice at the time was for a rigid left arm. He won his first British Open in 1896 and followed this with wins in 1898, 1899, 1903, 1911, and 1914. This record six wins is still unbroken.

James Braid was something of a slow starter when it came to winning Opens and was in his thirties by the time he collected the trophy in 1901. He quickly made up for lost time though, and by 1910 had won the British Open a further four times, in 1905, 1906, 1908, and 1910. When on form he was without doubt the best putter and had the longest hit of the three members of the Triumvirate. In his later years Braid became involved with course design and made quite a reputation for himself as a course architect. One of his best pieces of work must surely be the King's Course at Gleneagles.

J. H. Taylor was the first of the three golfers to come to prominence. He won the British Open in 1894 and, following Vardon and Braid's example, went on to win it a total of five times. A formidable opponent at any time, Taylor excelled in high winds because the characteristic low flight of his ball made his game less susceptible to such conditions than his contemporaries. In 1933 he was captain of Great Britain's victorious Ryder Cup Team. Taylor was also instrumental in the foundation of the first Professional Golfers' Association in 1901.

Huge crowds followed the trio wherever they played, and

Ryder Cup

By the 1950s the game had taken on a new status brought about by the financial rewards and, most important, the advent of television. There's no doubt Arnold Palmer was a superb golfer, but it was television that made him the first real golfing superstar as he played daily in millions of homes across America. The power of television also began to dictate game play including replacing the matchplay formula in professional tournaments with four rounds of strokeplay on separate days; players were now matched against the course rather than one another.

In the 1960s Arnold Palmer, Jack Nicklaus, and Gary Player, a South African, dominated the game, both on and off television. They became household names, even to people who knew nothing about golf, and were golf's first millionaires.

However, by the end of the 1970s the Europeans began to stage something of a comeback. In 1976 a young Spaniard burst on to the international golf scene. The nineteen-year-old Severiano Ballesteros emerged as a remarkable talent in his challenge for the 1976 Royal Birkdale Open. His form was impressive, and he captured the attention of the media and public alike with his easy grace and poise.

A few years later, in 1979, Ballesteros won his first British Open and then set about making his name on the American circuit. He did this with some style by winning the U.S. Masters, the first European ever to win the competition and, at twenty-three, the youngest champion in that tournament. Other

Europeans followed: Sandy Lyle won the British Open in 1985, while in the same year Germany's Bernhard Langer won the U.S. Masters. This revival of European golf climaxed with them winning the prestigious Ryder Cup that year.

The Ryder Cup is a biennial competition between British and American professional golfers, instituted in 1927. It had become something of a one-sided affair though, with America's success virtually unchecked until the British team was made the European team in 1979. Following their 1985 victory the Europeans went on to win again in 1987 and tie in 1989.

European players began increasingly to win on American soil, and in 1989 and 1990, England's Nick Faldo won the U.S. Masters, with Welshman Ian Woosnam following his example in 1991.

Arnold Palmer

The Future

❧

The impact of television and the superstar status of modern golfers continues to increase the popularity of the game. Golf has come a long way from its simple Scottish origins and golfers are now not only playing for prestige but for vast amounts of money and lucrative sponsorship deals.

In the last twenty years there has been a significant European revival in golf that coincides with the emergence of a number of notable European players on the professional circuit. The industry is particularly booming in Spain and Portugal, where resorts cater to the vast numbers of northern European golfers escaping their inclement winters to play in sunnier climes.

But the most significant expansion of the game has been in the Far East, particularly in Japan where today there are an estimated eight million golfers. There are over four thousand golf courses in Japan, but in a country where space is at a premium and demand far outweighs supply, joining a golf club can cost more than \$300,000. Consequently, although many Japanese golfers own a full set of clubs, as few as fifteen percent will ever play on a course. The others must be content with driving ranges like Tokyo's huge Shiba Park. The other alternative has been to look abroad. A number of the world's most famous courses, including Turnberry in Scotland and Riviera in the United States are now owned by Japanese corporations.

In addition, today's technology means that golf courses can be created almost anywhere, from swamplands to hillsides. Advances in landscape and irrigation techniques mean that perfect greens can be created in the middle of a desert. And the demand for golf is such that not only are such feats possible but they are in common use.

A notable example of such an achievement is to be seen at the aptly-named Desert Highlands in Arizona. The course was designed by professional golfer Jack Nicklaus and has been described as "a series of green footprints in the desert." It is certainly a remarkable, almost surreal course, which took Nicklaus over two years to plan.

Another Nicklaus course, designed in collaboration with Desmond Muirhead, is New St. Andrews in Tochigi, Japan. Located just outside Tokyo, the course is almost a showcase of technological advances. Caddies control a computerized electronic system which carries the players' golf bags while the golfers themselves are transported via a monorail. The course is also floodlit to maximize the availability of play.

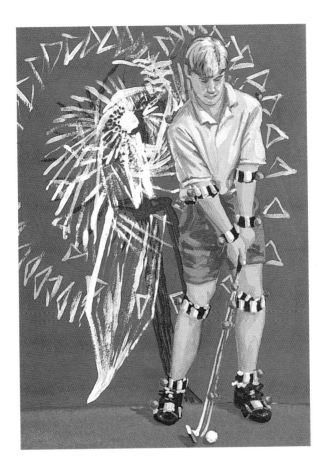

Technology has also had effects on the way golfers assess their performance. Once a golfer had only personal opinions (and usually those of a few golfing friends!) to figure out where his game was weak. Nowadays a golfer can hook up to a computer which will evaluate the subject's swing, stance and weight-to-power ratio. The USGA has invested over $2 million since 1991 to develop a computer program that systematically breaks down the process of a golf swing into a series of images, captured millisecond by millisecond, which are then portrayed on a screen for evaluation.

Likewise, golf balls now undergo tests similar to those developed to test the aerodynamics of cars. Materials such as thermo-plastics and other equally innovative substances are already important in the production of both golf ball covers and cores.

Golf clubs are also a short step away from being perfected by computer. The invention of the long putter, which has been met with equal amounts of criticism and adulation, is one such example. Others include the use of "square grooves" on the club face of irons to give greater stopping ability to the flight of the ball, and "woods" with metal heads.

Purists, concerned that all the advances in technology will detract from the sportsmanship of the game, need not worry though. Golf's governing bodies and authorities are determined that skill be retained in the game and that any such "improvements" are not capable of ultimately ruining the sport.

Nor are the professional golfers keen on the replacing of technique with gadgets. As Gary Player was once heard to remark on the subject of golf innovations: "With all the stuff that's coming out, guaranteed someday, on an uphill hole, a player will say: "I don't hit the ball that long, switch on that fan behind me.""

He, like the countless numbers of weekend players who head to their local course for a round or two, knows that golf's real strength lies not in perfection, but in the pleasure it brings to millions around the globe.

Whispers of the Heart for the One I Love

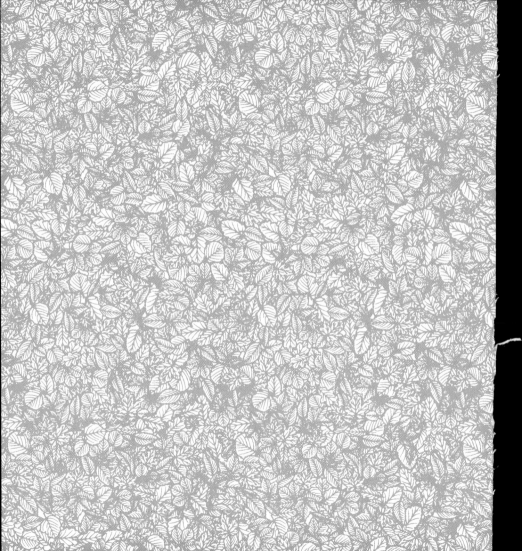

Whispers of the Heart for the One I Love

by
Richard Exley

Tulsa, Oklahoma

*T*o the One I Love

_____

_____

*F*rom

_____

_____

*D*ate

_____

_____

Whispers Of The Heart For The One I Love
ISBN 1-57757-200-3
Copyright © 1996 by Richard Exley
P.O. Box 54744
Tulsa, Oklahoma 74155

Published by Trade Life Books
P.O. Box 55325
Tulsa, Oklahoma 74155

Contents

 *for* **Brenda**

Little things mean a lot —
My favorite coffee mug,
"Your Body" by Kavanaugh,
a faded snapshot
capturing images of your childhood
from those distant days
before I knew you.

Little things mean a lot —
The way the sun
highlights your hair,
the love in your eyes
when you talk of your mother,
the sound of your laughter
when your sister calls.

Little things mean a lot —
Kerosine lamp light
bathing our bedroom
in honey-colored warmth.
The soft whisper of your voice
as you call my name
into the bedtime darkness,
a shared memory of by-gone years.

Little things mean a lot —
A love note in my briefcase,
a surprise call at mid-morning,
the touch of your hand in the dark,
the warmth of your back against
my belly as sleep seduces us,
the softness of your profile
against the pillow
in the first light of morn.

Little things mean a lot —
You are
all the little things,
and all the big things of my life.

"So Jacob served seven years to get Rachel,
but they seemed like only a few days to him
because of his love for her."
—*Genesis 29:20*

When
Love
Is New

Genesis 29:20

ascent Romance

"...show me your

face,

let me hear

your voice;

for your voice

is sweet,

and your face

is lovely."

— Song of Songs 2:14

Watching you walk

and seeing you smile

may not seem like much.

But for those of us

who have loved

from a distance,

waiting and hoping,

it is the heart's

consolation.

Things I'll Never Have

So much of my life
seems to be spent
wanting things
I'll never have.

A whole day
to spend with you
doing as we please.

An afternoon
for my fingers to play
in your hair.

An evening to
celebrate your smile,
an entire night for love.

Time enough
for your eyes
to say all the things
you can never put into words.

Like I said,
so much of my life
seems to be spent
wanting things I'll never have

If That Makes Me Guilty

Maybe

I shouldn't have rushed

into your well-ordered life.

Maybe

I should have left you secure

in your day-to-day business.

But I didn't,

and if that makes me guilty,

it's only of loving you.

Timid Love

I leaf through volumes of McKuen
and think of you.
I gave you "Stanyan Street"
and "Listen To The Warm" as the
first gentle gestures of my love.

You accepted them tentatively,
assimulating my love slowly,
almost as if you were afraid to
believe what you saw in my eyes.

I was afraid too,
that my love would go unnoticed
or that I might frighten
your timid love away.

Still,
I must have done something right,
because now you receive my gifts
and my love eagerly.

You

There are so many things

I like about you.

Little things

that are hard to put into words.

The way you hold your head

when you are lost in thought,

your smile when I surprise you.

Little habits,

things I've caught you doing

when you didn't know I was watching.

My mind's eye

forever winking them

into permenance.

Finally

*"His heart was
drawn to Dinah
daughter of Jacob,
and he
loved the girl
and spoke
tenderly to her."*

— *Genesis 34:3*

*You came into my life
softly and shyly,
afraid to believe
there was a place
in my heart
or in my world
for you.*

*Oh, but there was.
There was.*

Mid-Morning Surprise

The traffic light
turns red,
and I brake to a stop.
Casually I glance
down the street
and there you are,
half a block away,
dressed in red and blue,
your dark hair framed
against the bright
summer sky.

I watch
until a doorway swallows you.
The traffic light turns green
and impatient drivers
lay on their horns,
but I ignore them.
My mind has room
only for you
and a thankfulness
for a mid-morning surprise
dressed in red and blue.

Love Messages

I'm not lonely anymore

except when we're apart

or seperated

by a room full of people.

Even then

it's not the same.

Your eyes

send coded love messages

that I receive

a hundred heads away.

Cotton Candy World

Outside
naked branches
silhouette against a dull sky.
In shaded places
gray smudged snow show
the last traces of winter
hanging on.

Inside
kerosine lamp light
reflects off of a red telephone,
and my mind is in
a kind of cotton candy world
of sunshine and flowers
and you.

"Your cheeks are
beautiful with
earrings
your neck with
strings of jewels"

— *Song of Songs 1:10*

26

I Love You

Apart or together

I love you.

In a crowd or alone

I love you.

Be it day or night

I love you.

Right or wrong

I love you.

PART TWO

When Love Is Lost

Song of Songs 5:6

"I opened for my lover,
but my lover had left;
he was gone.
My heart sank at his
departure."
— Song of Songs 5:6

Only Me

I guess

I've always known

that the best

I had to give

was only me,

nothing more.

Somehow

I thought it was enough.

I'm sorry

if you expected something more.

Mismatched

Who would have ever believed
that we would get together?
You with your silliness
and sunshine,
Me with my melancholy moods
and shadows,
But we did,
and for a time
we had it all!

Who would have ever believed
that we could not make it last?
Not you,
with your ever present optimism.
Nor me,
with my dogged determination.

But we could not,
and after a time
the parting was all
we had left.

Who would have ever believed
that it would end like this?
You going your way,
me going mine,
still very much in love,
but unable to find
what it was we once shared.

Bt end it did,
and once more I am alone with
my melancholy moods
   and shadows,
while you roam the world
   in search of love,
disguised in your silliness
   and sunshine.

Like In A Game

It started, like in a game,

with neither of us thinking

beyond the next move.

We exchanged gestures

and glances,

timid overtures,

toward further intimacy,

without ever allowing

ourselves to consider

what was happening

or where it might end.

Looking back

it seems so foolish,

these misdirected efforts

to fool ourselves.

Who were we kidding?

We both knew

this game was for keeps.

Each succeeding move

involved us more deeply,

until our lives were so emotionally entangled

that nothing had meaning

except the passion we shared.

Now it's over,

like in a game

which has gone on too long,

and the painful untangling of our lives

is all we have left.

Classic Co-dependents

I smiled a lot
but not with my eyes.
No one seemed to notice
until you did and responded
out of a sadness of your own.
Then we came together.
Two misfits
fleeing the uncomprehending crowd.

Classic co-dependents were we,
feeding on each other's need.
For a time
it seemed enough,
but after awhile
even the sadness we shared
couldn't keep us together.

Still,
when you went away,
a part of me died.
We were destroying each other,
and you had to go,
but that doesn't seem
to make it any easier.

Even now,
you are often on my mind,
and I hope you've found
a real love.
Me?
I smile a lot,
but not with my eyes.

Friends or Lovers

Slowly,
little things first,
gestures of affection
carefully couched in friendship.
Weeks went by,
then months,
two years and more,
while our love grew,
a secret,
even from ourselves.
Disguised as comfort,
positive strokes given gently,
lest we should go too far too fast.
Once acknowledged, however
we couldn't go far enough,
fast enough.

Too late,
we realize that our love
has become a victim of our haste.
Too soon our love
is just a bittersweet memory,
a painful reminder
of what happens when friendship
is sacrificed for love.

How Do You Remember Me?

Everyone is gone,
and night has come to stay
until day returns
I listen to the ticking
of the antique clock
on the mantle,
sip espresso from a
demitasse cup,
and think of you.

I remember you
the way I saw you last—
walking across the street,
hurrying to get out
of the rain,
never looking back.

How do you remember me?
Half asleep
with my hair in my eyes?
Hungry mouth seeking yours
before I've brushed my teeth?
Eager hands
drawing you close?

I remember you,
    Always.
How do you remember me?
    Often,
I hope.

Without You

Without you my song
has no lyrics,
and my music
has no beat.
Without you my days
have no light
and my nights
have no end.
Without you my past
has no meaning
and my future
has no purpose.
Without you...Dear God,
without you
I have nothing at all.

Old Habits

I do all the old things
that once made life
come out right.
I listen to music,
thumb through familiar poetry
and write.

Still,
I keep hurting,
and it grows worse every day,
because I know
that while you may come back,
you won't ever stay.

Love Sick

Six months of sunsets,
and half a continent's breadth
haven't diminished my love for you.
If anything
they've only aggravated it.

Time was suppose to heal, all this,
but it hasn't.
I'm still
tattooed by your touch,
indented with the evidence
of lying close to you
so often for so long.
Even my mind
is shaped to fit your memory.

Still,
if loving you
has deformed me,
then let me be
an invalid for life.
Let time take its
healing hands
someplace else.

ieces of the Past

Small rooms
darkened by drawn drapes
and cloud covered days.
Beds rumpled
and unmade,
messy evidence of our presence.
A brown notebook
of personal poetry
containing recorded memories
and the commandments of love
that we developed
and made work for us.

With these and other
pieces of our past,
I'll make it through
this shapeless morning
and maybe even
find my way
back to you.

Gone, But Not Forgotten

There are not enough friendly smiles

in all the world

to erase yours.

Not enough warm arms

to make me forget

the love we shared.

Not enough love

to free me from the things

you made me feel.

Remembering

Outside
night descends,
and the snow drifts down,
wrapping the world
in a silent blanket of winter white.

Inside
music plays softly,
and I remember you
lying on my bed
moonlight crawling across your face
and love in your whispered words.

PART THREE

When
Love
Is True

Song of Songs 8:7

I'll Be There

"Many waters
cannot
quench love;
rivers cannot wash
it away.
If one were to give
all the wealth of
his house for love,
it would be
utterly scorned."
— Song of Songs 8:7

For you,
the thought of a life-long
commitment
is nearly as terrifying as death.
You wage a war within,
making your hand-framed face
an expressive portrait.
Trembling you ask,
"Do you love me truly?
Will I be able to count on you
when the tough times come?"
I smile an answer
and gently brush a tear
from your damp cheek.

Taking you into my arms
I whisper,
"I love you truly,
and when the tough times come
I'll be there."

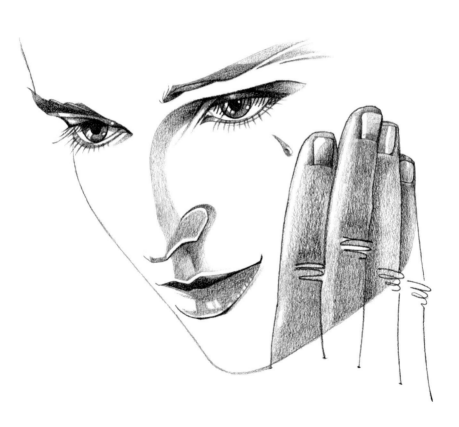

Marriage

For a long moment
we hold each other motionless
with our eyes.
I am surprised
by your eagerness.
You are frightened
by the greatness of my need.
Then timidly,
gently,
we come together,
and the gift of love
makes us one.

"*Come, my lover, let us go to the countryside,*
let us spend the night in the villages.
...there I will give you my love."
— *Song of Songs 7:11, 12*

The First Night

On the night stand
a single candle burns
casting a warm glow.

The quilted cover is folded back
and I lay on the bed waiting.
Soft music and perfume
permeate the air
as you enter the room
accompanied by the whisper
of satin and lace.

After all the years
the waiting is finally over
and now you slip into bed beside me.
Tenderly we give ourselves to each other
and our aloneness is lost
in the soft merging of our flesh.

Did I Ever Tell You?

Did I ever tell you
that I love you
early in the morning
with your toothpaste kisses
and your sleepy eyes?
With your headaches and
grumpiness
that only goes away
if I hold your hand
and whisper the soft things
you like to hear?

Did I ever tell you
that I love you
at mid-afternoon,
during coffee-break time,
when clocks and
crowded cafeterias
make smiles and warm hands
love's best language?
Did I ever tell you
that I love the way
you smell after a bath,
that I love the way
you feel in bed beside me,
that I love the way
you look after I've loved you?

Did I ever tell you
that I love you?
I do,
  I do,
    I do.

Contentment

*I sit here
in the near darkness
of a late rain-washed afternoon.
Thunder growls in the distance,
drowning out the sound
of the softly falling rain.*

*Yellow light from the kitchen
spills into my mostly dark study,
and I hear you banging pans
and humming softly.*

*I feel contented,
but I can remember
when it wasn't so.*

*When my life was mostly
sadness and shadows,
before the yellow light
of your love came spilling in.*

*Now my life is mostly sunshine,
and what sadness remains
huddles in the darkest corners
unacknowledged,
unless you are unhappy
or away.*

Day Demands

Predawn darkness gives way
to pale morning light,
and the small night sounds are
replaced by the noise of day.

In this moment,
I hate the light
and the day demands
that drive me from our bed.

In this in-between time,
after the night and before the day,
I worship the warmth of your arms
and the nearness of your body
sculptured in shape to mine.

It's only a fleeting moment
and even now the wedge of time
drives me from our bed
and into my sweater and shoes.

Standing and
watching you lost in sleep,
I'm consumed with loneliness.
Just seconds ago
I was secure,
a prisoner of your arms.

Now I'm leaving
to face the day
without you.

A Gentle Love

You've given me so much —
more than I ever imagined possible.
Simple things but rare —
a quiet place away from the noisy
world,
a gentle love without demands,
inspiration without expectations.
Common things too,
of uncommon value —
a cup of coffee
when I come home at night,
a fire in the fireplace,
supper on the stove.

I give you me,
  now and always.

I am yours
in a way no one else can ever be yours.
I will love you all the days of my life.
When you are lonely,
I will comfort you.
When you are tired,
I will refresh you.
When you are sick,
I will care for you.
I will share all your joys
and sorrows your whole life long.
We will celebrate growing old together;
warmed against winter's chill
by the memories of a lifetime
cherished and shared.

Only Love

Let others chart the course

of their lives

by the number of days

that come and go.

Our lives are charted by love.

They know no beginning or end,

no past or present,

no yesterday or tomorrow,

only the availability

or absence of love.

After Loving You

If ever I am tempted

to fall in love again,

I'll remember

that after loving you

there could never be

anyone else.

PART FOUR

A Final Poem

Ruth 1:16-17

"...Where you go I will go, and where you stay I will stay.
Your people will be my people and your God my God.
Where you die I will die, and there I will be buried.
May the Lord deal with me ever so severely,
if anything but death separates you and me."
— Ruth 1:16, 17

Love Remembered

If ever you are sad
and people treat you badly,
remember that once
there was a man
who saw you as you are
and liked what he saw.

If ever you are having a bad day
and you are tempted to doubt yourself,
to wonder if you will ever know
the love your heart seeks,
remember that once
there was a man
who loved you just the way you are

When the lonely nights come,
as inevitably they must,
listen again to the gentle things
he said to you.
Remember his tenderness
and his love.
Let your memories
keep you through the night.

And never forget
that when he went away
he left his love
for you to wrap up in
to help you through
all the winters of your life.

Other Books by Richard Exley are available at your local bookstore.

Straight from the Heart for Christmas
Straight from the Heart for Mom
Straight from the Heart for Dad
Straight from the Heart for Graduates
Straight from the Heart for Couples
How to be a Man of Character in a World of Compromise
Marriage in the Making
The Making of A Man
Life's Bottom Line
Perils of Power
The Rhythm of Life
When You Lose Someone You Love
The Other God – Seeing God as He Really Is
The Painted Parable

Tulsa, Oklahoma